Wake Up from Hereditary Trauma!!!

Discovering what is not mine to own. Hereditary ideas taught as demoralizing acts. Self-worth unaccountable.

By

Shana Rising A New

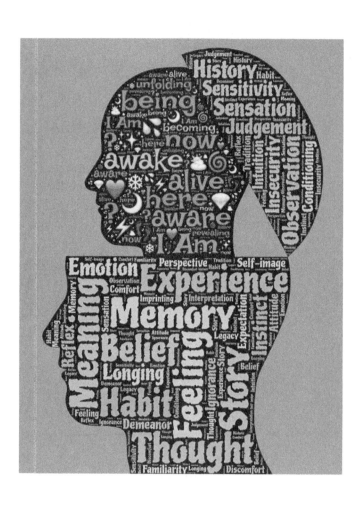

COPYRIGHTS

Fake Clowns... Acknowledgment

Thank you to all family, friend, foe, lover, heartbreakers, cruel life makers, false God believers, Santeria energy steelers, masked abusers.

Projected onto my life you have given me the opportunity to challenge the energies sourly encouraged. Not only touching my life, also for others who are voiceless, created by devils energy.

A steppingstone, ruthless lawyer I will be, humanitarian, social justice enthusiasts. Your thoughts reflect the being of you as a collective.

This is my day through universal encouragement and protection. Negative being of you as a collective tormenting my soul, existence touching skin, bruised wounds, bleeding heart, vomit filled bucket of your secrets.

Behold the unknown, dirty souls ready to be cleansed. Destroyer. Warrior being, universal leading. Lightworker, soul searcher, ready to share my god given gifts with the world.

Unapologetic, this book is just the beginning. **Your secrets will be unkempt!!!!**

About the Author

Shana Rising A New is a young woman growing and leading a future for her unborn children. Healing the path of old hereditary wounds programmed due to generational circumstances out of her control. Acknowledging the struggles, she endured in a life not of her own. Faith, awakening, meditation, and prayer self-taught expressing her hearts desires on a journey through universal law of attraction flowing in higher consciousness.

Future endeavors are achievable advocacy will be unapologetic for persons with disabilities, mental health, addictions including the modalities of social injustices. Soon to be a humanitarian enthusiast building a career in social justice protecting the voiceless challenging unjust human behavior in disrupting public health.

Words unspoken that will unleash educational resources that deconstruct programmed and comfortable behavior taught healing stigmas tarnishing indifferent societal normality.

The importance for space between universal energy waves challenges everyday livelihood; however, faith universally deconstructing programmed thought patterns negatively enforcing old cycles, reprogramming new evolution.

A volition ionization waiting to give life, corpuscle within the walls of humanity, the tree of life is procreating in the womb, blessings gifted in sacred touch, divine love, infrastructure evolves.

Lessons learned on a journey supplied to aid evolving **Divine Feminine** acknowledging healing insecurities. Embracing the irrelevance once betrayed self-worth is the key to all human life. What are the lessons you choose to embrace deprogramming lineage diarrhea cramping one's lifestyle?

Bathe in the light of self-resilience protecting your every being of sole purpose, that is you and your existence. All focus should solely be on you. The importance hidden an exterior growing beneath inner existence.

About the Book

Be your authentic self-releasing all the circumstantial misleading's and chaotic life that has entered a dark place where all wounds of pain buried disrupting psychological health. Finding love carrying hope in her heart creating conscious actions as waves vibrationally a force of light within God's child. She can no longer lead without the knowledge of higher consciousness.

Struggling with fears enlightened slightly touched by divine grace expressing the very being of self no more wondering what her sole purpose is in this life, the next, and forward.

NOT A VICTIM. NOT A SURVIVOR.

An ACHIEVER of circumstance not defined by another's toxicity created to hurt. Projected grief acknowledged through self-healing because this chaos is defined not hers to own.

Subjective oppression suppressed by controlling abuse of all forms beneath hidden truths shunned to be authentic self. Finding her Beacon of light shining brightly flowing through the heart of God's creation.

Epiphany embracing the life struggles emotionally triggered, I once feared, healing the piercing wounds a superpower molded into freedom, speaking my voice, sharing my story. Hope my words of truth will challenge the stigmas using my book releasing a soul purpose guiding new life for myself and my future family.

Healing has been a long journey, recently diagnosed with PTSD (Post Traumatic Stress Disorder) from childhood encouragement, taught to cope, instead of releasing chaotic energy.

Challenging life can be overwhelming facing the very existence for vibrational waves drawing in detrimental life forming changes within healthier alternatives. Living freely once held by the chains of hereditary cords. Low vibrational ego suggests escalation, the toxicity swirling inside the walls, tugging self-defeat.

Education is a defining moment when a person steps back and says no more of this corpuscle heredity bullshit. The never-ending turmoil imposed upon human life passed down from one person to another.

New creation is the thought process of reprogramming one's lineage, ways taught to be self-destructive, self-defecting never once taught, expressing inner peace. Sanctity for healthier psychological wellness.

AWAKENED CENTER

Perfection

Steppingstones in life are exceptional when discovering a new layer of self, you never expected to rise from the ashes of a phoenix revolting the chains once binding inner soul being.

The detrimental steps are leading forward with universal law of attraction. Fear no more we are as a collective everything that is life beneath these old barriers set to destroy a human soul by affecting public health showing psychological warfare.

Self-destructing patterns taught in unhealthy living accepting what is and what should as a social normality the lacking the teachings for self-worth.

Are you awakened to your self-worth as a collective? Public health is demolishing at a human cost, demoralizing a collective thought process.

We are taught through hereditary teachings we are perfect, to be perfect, spell right, speak right, look this way, what is and is not acceptable. When will change accountability for the teachings not of your own beliefs and wellness?

Self-destructing patterns, **NO MORE!!!**

How to use this Book

Utilizing this book is key to growing your higher consciousness, freewill solely for the **AWAKENED**. Sometimes when someone hears another's truth their authentic purpose ignites a fire within their belly (solar plexus fire) addressing the very issues causing turmoil.

The desire for freedom releasing an exponential aspect of self-evolving courage. An open path, standing for flexibility, the importance of one who navigates the twists and turns of life. Stiff, painful **ankles** mean change is difficult for you.

You are one who digs your heels and resists moving forward. The more life forces change upon you, the deeper you dig in, authentication is necessary as an aspect to live and not live to survive.

Survival is wearing a mask, pleasing a negative part of falsehood taught, projecting another, is a thought process oppressing you, inner child ready to blossom beneath the muck of chaos, cycling life's pain.

When does one stop and awaken, epiphany:
enough is enough? Change is now, altering living,
mind suggesting it is essential to a heart awakening.

Trusting universal law through prayer, hope and
faith in strength, healing, adjusting divine
intervention created by you. The All in greater sole
purpose consciousness love. Is this you?

Allowing yourself to open heart space entrusting
sole purpose, your true hearts desires addressing
fulfillment within Universal attraction. What you
create is you, is the attraction of good light, interior
self-worth entwined higher consciousness.

Note: Education is important as you read this
book, highlight contents that stand out the most to
you calling on your heart, take notes, define words
you don't understand or forget the meaning (I do).

Cry if you need to and write down what pains your
heart, throw it away, rip it up, toss it in the ocean,
dissolving away all that was.

Yes, it may feel cruel and hard, this is the new
beginning of your journey, training wheels

readjusted, the Universe's lessons for growth, healing puss filled wounds.

These words are suggestive. Be curious, learn, explore. It is scary, I know, I am on this journey battling those old, programmed thoughts hereditary driven.

HIGHER CONCIOUSNESS:

A Spiritual Path is Educating the Process to Awaken Self-Awareness.
Healing Wounds of Hereditary Trauma

Accountability/Responsibility
(Self-Growth)

Growth is the key aspect of life overlooking accountability acknowledging vibrating pain collected family trauma generational karma held on passed down too many births lived leaving behind misconception residue.

Old beliefs of acceptance occur when the **BYSTANDER EFFECT** (a traumatic occurrence that does not apply to another's life dismissing a witnessed event will be harmful for a human being, humanity). Incest infiltrates everyone's household Urban and Suburban communities all hide unforeseen discrimination.

Psychosis entails a severe disorder ensuring life acceptance is countable creation lineage beliefs inner childhood wounds internalizing faults subjective projections of hate enticing destructive behavior falsehoods entwined.

Intelligence outweighs unjust behaviors, inexcusable, penetration targeting an infrastructure of a child's mental barrier, safely unaware of the danger's lying, slithering around, dark energies striking at the most innocent moment of childlike behavior, God willing.

Post-Traumatic Stress Disorder (PTSD) formation residue loss of breath holding head above water trying to understand energies targeted against one's sole purpose in life stressing nonexistent truths. Is if funny when someone discusses topics such as domestic violence, sexual abuse, addictions, human sex trafficking, mental health, disabilities that are taught to be comfortable behavior. Among the issues unscathed by societal norms adjusted for someone's liking.

Experience suggest we cannot challenge the stigmas we all have created for each other as a human race. We are all responsible for the existence of self, self is The All as Life and Mind solely living acceptance of closed wounds once bleeding puss.

Fear based lies undone self-soothing all outcomes choosing conscious love, God's presence no longer soles searching encouraging words of defeat projectile vomit toxic burning skin deep.

Sticks and stones, cutthroat deep embedded wounds reality words do hurt and burn into one's soul bearing pain driven puss dripping with intention destroying reassurance undeniable rejecting prosperous ascension.

Life exception not valued disguised by another is defining reliance on words killing the corpuscle a beautiful soul. Expressing escape chained tangled cords toxic abbreviation of understanding pain shouted protecting my barriers.

Afraid of touch by conscious love will it stay or go, defeat selfless deserving of you. Rejection implies all the above life's downfalls around every corner awaiting crumpling heart digesting defeat. Living mind struggling to stay afloat head above treacherous waters drowning massacre of joyous prayers.

Lightning strike vibrating fear-based patterns struggling to breath releasing existence heart shaken touch unthinkable. Justification belief emotional shut down debriefing self-mutilation disempowered womanhood inner child slowly

flowing within the universal vibration adjusting to creations ability aiding heart felt plea.

HELP heal the little girl inside hidden in darkness unsafe to the eye!! Call out, cry's heard millions of light years away sounds booming at all energy levels. Can we hear our voice as sound wave frequencies milli hertz calculations as we speak to the universe weeping in despair?

All have heard my call. Frightening tailspin how universal law seeks your higher consciousness forced wages through self-resilience a breathing life releasing puss filled wounds of darkness.

Shouting STOP, I do not want you here!! Protecting my heart from pain afraid belief driven reoccurring cruelly judging myself and divine masculine a possibility awaiting in the far distance.

Could this be true? I do not know. The unknown never shares blessings in disguise never believing blessings could be afoot with all the turmoil created for I, circumstantially.

Circumstantial residual cords never letting go of pass hurts dreading what could be around the corner before the occurrence. Acknowledging I am creating this negative entity based on old patterns pass down as an inheritance I do not have to accept.

Boundaries!!! Psychosis filled rage anger fearing change will be useless even though life has exhausted every turn on my own. The universe has my back still trying to embrace this conscious love afraid to be alone unwed mother frightened in the circumstantial let down of self-reassuring goal protecting emotionally unsafe a survival skill left undone.

Survival driven soul seeking franchise out of touch based solely on monetary foundations. Funds bleeding the lifeless weaknesses only visioning the answers outsourced instead of inner sole answering meditation addressed chaotic unbalanced energy ping ponging ego vibrations vomiting puss filled cyst ready to pop.

Drainage filled bowls deepening in muck anger shouting will this be real! Pinching my skin asking pleading prayer why this had to happen. Not victim. Brutalizing loathing in dismay stressing heart felt pain all I ever knew.

Why should any human experience pain continuing to believe this does not have an ending. Endings of old cycles are new beginnings evolutionary beauty on the horizon expressing conscious love in the unknown unspoken words secretly expressed.

Enthusiastic love touching the lives of all majestic creatures are human creation. Creation is the realization we are the universal law attracting fighting our true existence amongst Mother Earth.

Mother Gaia mother of all are sacred beings without co-existence, we will never find peace only pain puss filled wounds inherited identity driven virtue mistaken.

Finding choose wisely feared never lasting love education is a key element founded on growth justified by conscious love universally enforcing strength adjusted in faith.

Never fear change occurring new opportunities and beneficial healing. Rejection only lies in the heart when allowed self-mutilating habits scratching at the surface believed falsehoods inherited residue.

Psychosis

Mental barriers broken down struggling to find the daily aspect of being key elements to success in life is emotional balance vibrating at a higher frequency.

Journey finessing challenging preventing growth psychosis filled thoughts weaving through lineage landfilled patterns, mindset, childhood toxicity inherited.

Encircling feeling dizziness fighting the existence of being building stronger mental state considered unstable judgmental projections self-mutilating. Chaos theory battles walls crumbling defeating the purpose of sole plain, suicides breathing energy life useless.

This theory creates an onlook healing psychosis spinning leading to detrimental baggage left behind circumstances not of your control old beliefs and faith.

It is this evolution of domestic violence, sexual abuse, addictions places of darkness hiding pain.

Driven diagnosed a severe mental disorder in which thought, and emotions are so impaired contact lost with external reality. Diagnosis medically presuming labeling symptoms addressing coping mechanisms supposed one but not for another. If one lineage labeling a cycle filled falsehood infiltrating the body a vessel corpuscle oocyte embedded in the womb vibrating.

Deceased, sparse controlling families growing filling motherhood and fatherhood. Accountability where it may be why continue lead with a dying breed. Life encourages healing so many opportunities universal law given guided angel's unseen breathing touching inner soul.

Education supplied utilizing content driven understanding higher consciousness more so seeking healing withholding self-resilience. Paring all content addressing PTSD (post-traumatic stress disorder), embracing emotional understanding no outburst taking in self-taught conscious love deprogramming mass media beliefs governmental fears and struggles.

Foliage stress roots corded entwined in hearts connection bearing all truths written dialogue portrayed as life lineage not of mine to own foreseen faults forgiveness and betrayal sabotage dreams chaotic downfalls, catch me please. No safety net psychosis feeling unsafe alone believed not loved in existence live life, survival not of your own circumstance. Dropping all holds, setbacks no more.

Living Mind infinite worthiness addressing the mental transmutation of psychosis fulfilling your energy wave a diagnosis scientifically assumed. Titles and labels create damaging faults adding to the stressors of life Psychotherapy and Psychology, need be altering patterns healing wounds instead to profit.

Yes, the use of these resources can be beneficial however clinical patients run away shutting down by bias content ignorant to their own faults career ideology. Brainwashed medication is the belief system we all need what if we inherited a new wave of vibration penetrating the old bull taught process programmed as PSYCHOSIS, Psychology Science.

Objectifying one's soul encourages the very existence tolerating outburst taunted beings

projected hate frustrating pain that is not yours. Enraged process fighting protecting life unborn no more for you to hold. Parents driven nail on head biting their skin touching life teetering on edge drunk addicted abusive psychosis.

Worthiness unveiled spiraling fists incest touched bathing in disgust shame unaware of faith healing puss filled wounds. Punching bag stand still what is it to you fist wielding basket case psychosis mental health questioned unstable processed belief inherited barriers chiseled crumbling bitterness afoot.

Labyrinth vibrating patterns unknowingly shaken footprints projectile sticks and stones pressing the frontal lobe suppressed accessing all blinded infinite living mind. How to escape its effects upon us, sourcing old wounds growing in strength adjusting to use it do not fight the current wavelength.

Instead the old dirty footprints leaving residue dancing around taunting playing with ego. Psychosis on a field trip vomiting fear body shaken with stress mental anguish. Mental Alchemy swirling in despair believing truths fear releasing God like healing treacherous reins.

Illumined souls reverently receiving spirit grossed actions upon self, guidance vibrating all around shouting *let me help you.* Spirit is you your soul yelling screaming asking for help hard journey confused miracle child given not received. Heartfelt joy despairingly frightened worried unborn seed ill unseen.

Trustworthy faith driven beneath the exponential life frozen in time afraid knowingly asked to receive truth understanding there is more to

life than I, you, child rearing. Universal access afoot, palms held out given needs rewarded because I agreeing to self-journey with unborn seedling venturing ruthless empowered for the unjust.

Disempowered no more teeth grinding silence enabled frontal lobe vibrating third eye connecting source filled god conscious love. New beginnings psychosis unraveling fear-based ego teetering unsteady light shining upon darkness chaos-stricken roots uprooted projectile facing beauty my heart's desire prayers answered unforeseen.

Holding arm's length opportunity nonsense filled self-pity spirals God angels looking down shaking head *Come on Shana get with it.* Finishing book embracing content acknowledging beauty stress free frequency higher consciousness no more pain. Psychosis be gone bug spray prepared mosquito bitten itching.

Surface Qi Gong entitled privilege excepted new head space balance inquiry releasing heart anger adrenaline rush breathing resilience energy tingling pulsating through my veins upholds existence blessings in disguise.

Emotional Burnout = (Fear of Men/Tyrant)

Tyrant inflamed heart aching hyperventilating watery eyes bearing all violent words. Frequency raising exuberant calmness no longer need to battle warrior like pain holding onto unnecessary projectile vomit. Escaping the grips of falsehoods carried agelessly through life unknowingly expecting miracles preparing life as we know, not programmed to be.

Matrix parallels enticing warping theologies infused bull shit addressing womanhood as if your knowledge precedes you. Voiceless bystander seeing penetrating structural damage bits and pieces binary to self visionless psychosis ingestion.

Loneliness begs upon fear based heartfelt sorrow least trustworthy punching body structure life almost gone lifeless body tasting blood ribs broken punctured lung gasping crying for air. Voice of calmness motherly love bright yellow light warm hand on wound healing internally. God spoken angels healing savior amongst me childhood of ten frightened the unexplainable happened miracle risen beneath darkness.

Touch by the grace of God creation all naming who I am Queen universally protected. Moments of tears unintentional weeping bewildered life saved confused sole purpose ungrateful betrayal of self-hearts awoken

on knees pleading why unbearable struggle life in existence.

What is strength lying dormant afraid to sleep hitting pain vibrating bone structure tormented and abused grossly touched creeping chaotic driven anger. Parental abuse projectile demons sounding

howling growling pot filled hate trinkets name on paper Santeria less phased untouchable careless configuration. Controllable circumstance childbearing no parental supervision inherited shame motherless daughter unloved no knowledge cleansing conscious love.

Timeless discrepancies small window to conscious motherhood loved hopeless melted away heartbroken discouraged wielding knife fist pounding distinguished worthiness family secrets unraveling secretly within universal hand.

Powerless battles confrontation spiraling out of control punching bag tossed around hair pulling teeth shattering jaw broken dangerously low suffocation. Judgements placed where need not be God driven heart conscious, love secretly awaiting believed to be out of touch tumbling down hill asking where divine masculine is.

Will he speak his truth? Shedding fear of men tyrant dictatorship skin shedding old wounds bruised bones will divine masculine see my beauty hear my whispers pampering holding back not letting go of hand infinite living mind togetherness immortality conscious universal being, my existence.

Dredging ponds muck filled paralysis fearful touch shaking lifeless battles men at a distance do not worship sacred divine nectar father you have made me afraid to be Queen bee.

Divine masculine does not deserve my discretion judgement fell on my heart forgotten passed pain maturity untrue believed to be Casanova bastard seeds planted towns multiplied siblings unknown not sacred to me. Self-image ovum falling rock bottom drowning despair fear

anger vibrating shouting screaming losing sanity struggling voices calling frightened confused I thought this would never be.

Protected heart needing walls to tear down please chisel broken wounds defeated divine masculine were barriers hide prove me wrong facing truth that is you, unforeseen before but was not sure I knew my worth was it with you.

Thoughtless hopelessness single motherhood divine masculine welcomed embracing family that is of I, is to be ovum from another could this be a possibility transition transmutation teach me to be you. Your vibration holds me do not let me go, go move forward we are a solid package will you shared our life in Unity.

Infinite conscious love immortal to the human eye programmed falsehood of a maturity portrayed inherited accountability disappearance of Houdini. Speak truth your heart's desire here with me addressing your existence.

Even if I do not know who you are knight in shining armor, king entailed self-made manhood empowered understood frequency tingling euphoria ecstasy pill adrenaline flowing through our veins divine nectar engorged love where might you be.

Throat chakra let it vibrate you acknowledge communication endlessly. Kissing infinite living mind hidden beneath divine masculine prove me wrong you exist universally creation that may be do I create you leading me hand in hand.

Generational happiness creates King that be I your Queen mother of your seedlings to be tree of life womb healing binding hold touching sky Thoth knowledge peek a boo surprising you visible unknown generated discretely.

Life: New Beginnings

Acceptance {Psychological Health}

Health is a body function balancing conscious awareness realigning with the wave of self-healing allowing acceptance for a journey. Fall in place focus on growth letting go of friction standing, being contributes to health mind, body, and soul. This also ends illness functioning among the multitude of ailments humanity suffers. Man creates mental finite vibrating planes unseen.

Mental components according to (Epicurus) ancient philosopher a successor of Aristotle, *illness*

*is the being of all living breathing life as you should
bestow the desires of a human being's heart.*

Experience created chaos vessel appealing
emotional breakdowns vomiting crying releasing
the pain felt within soul unconscious vibrating
wanting life fully complete letting go all that is not
of me, not mine to own.

Struggles appearing never ending mental health
shaky adrenaline junkie living off pain tightening
ahold of me conscious awareness battling inner
demons passed down inherited flowing through the
veins of another's creation.

Finite creation sticky residue vines entwined
dangling above and below plane calling upon divine
intervention sourcing all that is weapons of mastery
thinking heart yearning residual fading mental
images in your mind foliating life.

We are The All infinite altering trauma Post
Traumatic Stress disorder healing the wounds once
yielding loud booms violence of self, I not me. The
whole truth infinite power stress relieving
obnoxious sensory projectile vibrating a frequency

incoherent adjusting atmosphere the art of alchemy that is The All.

All being health cleansing trauma introducing Qi Gong balance calmness sole purpose womb healing abbreviating new beginnings seedling vibrating above and below. Privilege is bestowing life healing mental health not as the stigma societal configuration statistically vital systematic as only illness, not that it so.

Unbalanced mental health occurs when harm intentionally manipulates a human being creating continuous thoughts negatively inferring the flow of life. Accountabilities violently ill vomiting emotional pain injuring existence sabotaging tingling procreation according to whom.

Challenging the vitality inherited as beliefs and faith untrue to seedlings moving forthwith unto I, you, me. Acknowledge consciously aware breathing life into an unborn child ready to feel, smile, grow challenging societal norms that of all.

Whom are you to aid in a women's choice not of your decision we are creation only drawn in by sperm usage untouched by conscious love? Heal as written words to paper health is knowing you have addressed the being of self.

Hearts desires frail to breath live life not programmed survival. Divine intervention calling upon our vibration be true to you any one of you embraced in love. Loneliness hard lesson chiseling stubborn programmed ways masked behavior ego playing peek a boo.

Pounding frontal lobe fears memories of ill will against forbidden wavelengths less than of existence presently focusing on PTSD healing not coping mechanism (psychosis theology).

Detrimental teachings no more. Educational path acknowledging growth is lessons sending and countering new expectations challenging newer alternatives for healthier psychological wavelengths.

Presence

Moments passing journey sparring programmed patterns forcing self-growth embracing all access points relating to divine intervention fighting disbelief. Unknown change challenging the existence of all that was and now that is.

Toxic presence realigning conscious love barreling emotions outward suppressed anger misguided not present calmness alienated logic broken down this is not I, me, you. Fiddling hands shaken fueled adrenaline prosthetic limb impaling womanhood sacred to God. Divine presence sweet nectar warm to the touch insert lust driven smoking hot transitions do you see beauty.

Ego presence non-essential trustworthy fear angry chaos confused unintentional indecisiveness-based upon infrastructure nocturnal selfishness.

Disempowered beauty presence challenged obverting disastrous psychopathic killings red flags driven path shifted baby on the way inner child fears scratching skin intestines twisted battle cry's driven yelling screaming disembodied being.

Invisible prayers fire in belly existential powers unseen higher consciousness beneath rubbish traveling in and out of consciousness. Medically induced coma programmed beliefs obsolete divine paradox the whole truth of being man (context of human gender however so) creates mental finite.

Motivations higher truths (ascension) carried bubbles popped unforeseen out of touch falsehoods stupid thoughts overpowering self-awareness acknowledged disturbance unconstitutional prayer battling unnecessary arguments.

Illumined souls reverently: spirit risen solar plexus suffocation conjuring healing ego hopeless fighting ascension infinite power the art of alchemy. Education calming Qi Gong, energy balance joyous momentums unseen to the Divine counsel.

Evolution challenged by trust disempowered releasing encouragement writing this wavelength pass hurts no longer a category of study. Disillusioned fears processing expectations untrue to the heart lying ego giggling no power over me collective exponential beings unseen processing witchy trauma falling apart heart magic truths all that is will be unto you.

Relieved jokingly saying I was a fool I am not sorry for this journey this child blessed that be all driven beneath a process unanticipated blessing. Rubbing away old residue lessons healing progression targeting a sole wheeling suffocation heavy chested breathing feared based fishing drowning untrue to self-conscious love.

Fighting hearts desires unipositive ion charged oppression calming unbalanced curses built on terror. Death associated life appreciated fond awareness breathing polarity conscious love tumbling knocking on door closer than one believes.

Baby counting days of birth born into a new evolution rekindled love unconditionally protected being. Processing unthinkable science knowledge struggling uncommon to the human mind. Education prohibited ego-based fear secretly drips in nooks and crannies beautiful light, divine paradox.

Brazen tenacity encouraged lovable woman beautiful creator of life womb healing evolution vibrating ovum tickling all that is. Present being I embracing solutions provided by Universal counsel accepted divine masculine prayed among foundations thriving the impossible out of reach.

Self-loving habitat mother to be you. Precious life wings cleansed moving adjusting bone structure growing attaching vessel changing higher self-realigning earth-bound angel living life so.

Exercising Yoga, Qi Gong, accumulating divine polarity drawing in prayer mating call forever chi consciously vibrating the structure heart-based ascension advancing connecting links soul conditioning.

Presence healing old sores puss filled wounds violating vessel aspirations mind spinning out of control believing fear is the truth of all incriminating being. Joy parasite cords sucking life trembling triggers suffocating conscious love aggregation of electrons stop holding the world on your shoulders.

Give all speaking through divine paradox inspiration is in spirit knocking on your door here to help healing wounds lifting the blinders vibrating rapidly intensifying hardships thoughts furiously out of control ignoring help under the law of all, prayer.

Understanding presence transmutation effort challenging the norms of societal infantries' subservient laws created and designated martial to humankind. Fear-based organization barreling guns blazing singing praise to their ways poisoning zombie behavior intensifying the weapon of ability imprisoning will relief to be free from all that was, now is.

Gravitating formations atoms adjusting DNA sensory cells triggered bathing in light darkness fading in the distance absolute being divine paradox taking off training wheels letting you ride the wave a beautiful life everything is work and confidence.

Empowerment speaking your truths experience as it is in this book re-aligning taking back control of virtue once stolen innocent inner child being of evolution. Particles of force relieved to find resilience self-worth reassured, universally protected.

Mental planes foggy near-sighted despairingly scarce propitiate selfish needs for another vomiting betrayal untrustworthy fighting nowhere near who I am underestimated surprises in store for those untrue to humankind.

Beginnings of New Life without CHAOS

Acclimate

Immanent mind is all of consciousness betraying self-sole purpose acclimate adjusting new evolution foreseeing the existence of truth. Heart pounding adrenaline anxiety filled chaos overwhelming head frontal lobe vibrating accessing old patterns re-aligning panic.

Cruel intentions will become faded in the distance no longer accepting behaviors. Boundaries stronger than before sharp knives sticks and stones calmness analyzing energy unbalanced blinded once before no longer will be.

Franchise building principle of rhythm challenging unjust voiceless beings processing life changing gossip no longer target degree of knowledge no longer emotional broken down. Hateful stance barrels blazing ruthless queen ready for battle warrior sword wielding cutting all cords vines attached to life once in darkness.

Born storyteller life expectancy thought short breathless angel present touched vessel broken bones blinders lifted, I am an achiever of a circumstance not of my own. Domestic violence sexual abuse violent terrors sleepless nights unsafe to close eyes no longer scathing fear immobilization.

Emotionally broken always made to feel wrong being who I am guarding heart always wondered how long shielding life no longer need to fight. Misdiagnosis triggers challenged unsteady made to feel unbalanced broken-down mental barriers chiseling self-destructive victimhood left undone.

New evolution beauty acceptance that is universal law who am I to be all that is Queen bee embracing higher self-divine earth angel. Dusting off wing's stringy cords chains entangled holding down flight tipping weight so heavy breathless challenging warrior.

Cries feeling insecure passed wounds no longer exist darkness forgiven light driven prosperity unforeseen. Criteria gyrating formations atoms pulsating prayers connecting life existence worthy conscious love.

Wholeness completed shuffling cards dealing joy training wheels ripped off tricycling confidently womanhood motherhood proud.

Divine Feminine

Debilitating memory waves sharp words tearing away womanhood touch violating mindful aura self-taught respect pleasure of the unthinkable Queen. Questionable, doubting finesse respectable outburst tears flowing river filled anguish heart beating faster and slower. Strength irenic confidence shadowed sassiness cunning head held high achievements unacceptable.

Never embracing beauty light diminished hateful slurs ally building. Tarnishing an achiever brutally battered fighting off the devil holding life trying to feel valued loved battling existence no divine feminine nor masculine should feel less than valued.

Suicide flutters in and out of consciousness configuring plotting the details deriving being out vessel carrying life so much more to create existence is beautiful warrior like attitude fearless unjust behavior willing and able to set free truths unveiled hidden beneath buried piles of shit.

The divine masculine feminine energy vibrating gyrating womb stretching life living breathing never had a chance to be mom, Mother's Day, Father's Day, wife, husband, partner, team, dad faith assured.

Why is it not enough? What lies beneath all truths bearing seeing the existence of evolution conscious love secretly aligned observed?

Always made to feel her, Shana there is something wrong with you days. Walking in a daze blurry tears dripping down beauty wet face eyes swollen weeping screaming to the universe why do human beings choose unkindness.

What is the baffling concept of humanity? Questioning self-blaming again damaged friendships, relationships, family work, school, acquaintance, accomplishments am I a fool?

Truth tellers see trouble inner soul 'I am feared' brazen to address comfortability living in falsehoods brutal truths emotionally misunderstood challenging superiority attitudes.

Divine feminine warrior light worker battling shield wielding sword bright wings powerful illuminated with God's touch, necessity building infrastructure.

Attracting hate, feared by a handful loved by all (unseen) life is abstract facing all forms of spirituality. Enlightenment vessel brightening joy evoking calmness emotionless new beginnings without chaos leading with accountability seedling aspiring soul conditioning.

Lower ego of polarity the pendulum of moods and feelings darkness stepping into light. Higher ego elevated consciousness hail epiphany essential growing within the compounds of freedom.

Warriors are light workers Archangels battling the evils low vibrational energies of unjust behaviors as divine feminine struggles identity questioned self-doubting, can there be conscious love?

Am I self-sabotaging beneath all taught deprogramming tainted belief *All Men Are Bad All good ones are not for me or gay?* Divine feminine is the epiphany of man fumbling in stupidity voicing the undermining of being you, stop new creation.

Manifesto {not declaring murder}

Connecting links soul-conditioning eccentric individuals bathing in selfishness babbling hate despised structure nocturnal deviance pounding self-harm scratching skin punching falsehoods monster behavior manifesto livelihood dictatorship state of mind-controlled.

Wavelength capabilities changing perspectives of Socrates and Plato, the immortality of self is deceased dyer to being growth in achievement propels life in existence. Self-exploration endures treacherous roads fighting old beliefs tear through the soul freedom empowered hearts bonding sharping daggers thrown in direction of conscious love.

Faithfully giggling contemplation releasing battling inner demons' cords slithering entangled deep-rooted suffocation tingling aspirations penalty beliefs structure filled basement level addictions.

Body filled bubbling anger releasing selfless actions ready to rumble tumbling dirty clothes maturity questionable direct woman childhood darkness lifeless body ungrateful thought filled words over analyzing experienced purpose.

Buffoon clown jabbering life is good women trophies fearful repetition grossly close sanity driven madness questionable unscathed lawful actions depriving innocent sole purpose.

Derivative actions blood stained clothes mom hiding bloody eye hospitalization dislocated jaw, will this life be for me?

Manifesto altered bastard seed not my DNA bloodwork dripping XY chromosomes, genetics lacking education white skinned child dark skinned siblings those are mine illiterates drop out gang banging womanizer murderous douche bag.

Illness foreseen lacking the ability of cause and effect rubbing sores laughter ringing out the devil is DEAD!! Lies filled atmosphere feeling mislead betrayed by universal law, prays touching beauty he never challenged man's cruelty suffering existence are.

Fatherless hopelessness intangible laws advocacy half-witted blindness bystander effect breathing down my neck slave work scrubbing floors afraid to be alone devil hooves horns red skinned growling in dreams shivering from fear teeth chattering will I die today.

Childhood bearings fueled hate murderous plot pleading with universal law ignoring my cries faith lost anger self-blame God rearing why these parents of this life. Lifeless body trying suicide careless actions am I loved lying in bed drowning in liquor pills ingested pen to paper hateful words weeping.

Wet smudged ink on knees asking God for forgiveness will heaven accept me hell retrieved motionless body poking heel saved again. Fatherless mother unloved touched snaky hands defiled vessel transmutation soul lifting pieces torn higher awareness tiptoeing on eggshells.

Expectations of death miscommunicated. Universal law will nit allow me to die, not by other hands nor of my own.

Figuratively

Polarity equals consistency barrels filled emotions tugging war between falsehoods truths of being hearts desires shoveling holes burying self-loathing aspirations. Fading divine masculine an illusion hopeless romantic knight rescue on horse sweeping off feet only happens in fairytales dreamlike state of imagination.

Co-existence plain self-reassuring drumming drama emphasis carrying booming cries whaling vibrating intense heart pain overwhelmed asking why the feeling of loneliness always a kind heart to all humankind had figuratively speaking a divine relationship could exist.

Breathing techniques wings fluttering heaviness weighed down fear mongers attacking every dream façade inspired divine paradox touching base handing goodies shivering unbearable thoughts aggressively violently approaching surreal being none exist plausible possibilities opportunity infrastructure brazen conscious love.

Depicted story telling invisible thought process could life be so beautiful existing only in my heart anger filled emotions confusion does universal law work understanding grasping divine energy. Wasting time dancing on eggshells divine channeling offering cause and effect opportunities realigning sole purpose not figuratively speaking joy fear-based thoughts mental alchemy knocking on door.

Divine masculine consciously aware love making body touching yoni the center of all existence life's creation womb filling breathing releasing lineage trauma. Star gazing friendly soothing conscious love is not figuratively speaking truth seeking knocking at door typing healing universal law of attraction key to all desires.

Our aid with your will to believe acknowledge divine energy does and will continue to sprinkle essence grabbing all bullshit needing to end at once roughness enforced only in low ego vibration waves no sassiness here only enticing magical miracles entailing beautiful horizons of completeness living life to its fullness.

Peace within A Dimension Higher

Consciousness: Higher Being

This journal reflects self-awakening to growth occurring daily. Love & Light Be with You....

Merkabah {pictured above}, You Define!
Yoni (Sacred Nectar)

The Yoni is a temple gate, where the pure essence of a woman connected it is an opening into the holy womb, the birth space for all life. The Yoni is a great teacher, for a woman learns true self love, sovereignty, and self-respect by welcoming into her Yoni which is loving, trustworthy and honoring her true essence. The Yoni is the sacred doorway into a woman's holiest of all places.
-Hinduism

Sacred touch is an opportunity to be in the presence of Shana beauty all of existence challenging unjust friend family foe men who choose voiceless actions expressing love is their loss sharing multitudes expressing emotional nurturing wisdom aligned.

Growth in womanhood Maiden Mother Crone justifications beyond excuses clear to their ego no rejection here divine masculine if you love me take that leap of faith make up for time lost.

Expressionless motionless jiving jiggering in my presence conscious love curls toes Yoni warm and sweet. Womb filled ovum thriving ageless beauty timeless angel earth bound processing sole purpose lessons grabbing calmness.

Fish thrown back into sea so many pointless efforts Yoni rejection sacred touch unappreciated fishing gone wrong expectancy. Principle as of universal application good natured human being god like conscious love.

Unwilling men have no privilege here needing permission drawing in expression of discussing interaction sharing lives sacred being entwined truth driven fluorescent love, you and I will be family evolvement is all of wholeness. Left in the dark grotesque feeling do not know if divine masculine will be present sharing his engorged love.

Pleasant hearts filled joy creation womb vibrating oocyte releasing floating with pride baseless envy jealousy no time to stop stumper over spilled milk.

Embrace divine nectar offered through guidance universally connected conscious love rising anguish no more breathing into vessels entwined hearts fluttering beating loudly suggesting life to live existence within each vibration divine paradox appreciated healing useless residue left behind swine filled auras.

No touch!

A River that Flows is the life of a Peaceful Journey.
If Allowed by You and Me. Free from All that was,
old hereditary teachings.

Psychological Health:
Breaking Down & Barriers Stigmas,
Reprogramming Oppression

Judgements

Expectations disappointments materializing frantic conspiracies drumming pounding anger cruel illusions penetrating judgements decent human beings touching life breathing toxins kindness, chivalry to the unknown.

Lost in time selfishness desperation pulling up pants shamed bullied frightened in life challenges humans portray defeating sole purpose ignited fire match burning pain residual puss dripping from nooks and crannies dispositional point of views vomiting fluid diarrhea attitude baffling bitches douche bags of many.

Neither goal driven lighted path structure ready to crumble breathing life force ready to disperse powerful energy proven to be God send, angry frustrated no longer will be questioning life expectancy of another.

Sole purpose vibrating talking nonsense preparing chi not immobility stirring in trauma holding onto personal torment carrying vengeance hate mongers striving. Sucking anger unhealthy process leeching energy projecting, see no evil, speak no evil, hear no evil.

Divine blessings spoken standing still weighing the abuse unjust I give to myself fearing the life guided through divine counsel be the creator of this world, seedling.

Judgements despair reality channeling the acceptance of what is taught to be, think, and feel as comfortability, societal normality is believed to be true. Less judgement on self. Channel inner light truest of you.

Phantom Thoughts

Pultruding horns suspected devil's energy bathing lighting striking clock ding dong the witch is dead enemy lingering whispering words chanting hateful projections 'you are not my daughter you treat me like a dog I wish I never had you.'

Pain stricken drama held in vessel life expectancy short lived jealousy envy soaring vibrating tingling beneath wellness applauding proudly aspiration head held high no longer needing family drama ownership of no one tell tailing honoring falsehoods.

No longer my family shut up devil's energy you are not welcome here on this journey phantom thoughts created by you; parents not well enough to be human. Mental health deteriorates battling addictions biting nails breathless aspirations life chosen death (old patterns recycling trauma behaviors lineage aspirations) becomes illness.

Will you ever seek justice for soul bearing light driven peaceful state of mind awareness of higher elevation surrendering all that was now that is.

Spiteful antagonizing intentions projecting hateful itchiness, bacteria.

Parasite behaviors thank your chemical reoccurrence bug repellent you all are motherless fools. Washing off once inhabited leech pulling low vibrational energy protected aura divine purpose angels calling standing guard you longer hurt me accountability you will receive.

Discretion

Visible unapologetic God's creation always made to feel there is something wrong with me authentic ascension no longer wills be. What I wish I create what you reap I will sow wish unto you disastrous countability the principle of cause and effect however that may be.

Consequences ruthless I will be penetration skin deep aura cleansing angelic beings hand healing miracle opportunities driven words spoken. Frantic eggshells crunching tip toeing around me truth spoken undying anger victimhood wrung dry programmed beliefs falsehoods triggers pain healed not a people pleasure brown noise seeker.

Diligent worker inventive mind mental barriers solid emotionless class reaction calm discretion my ass societal norms bittering mindless sounds loss common sense withered bullshit pleasure zombie believers.

Creation

Resilience withheld fountain of youth creation womb filled aspirations speaking truths healing past life regressions scratching surface questionable behavior unkind to humanity.

Unjust driven passions tumbling beneath you washing hands of sticks and stones fighting old beliefs programmed brainwashed delirium traveling buffoons circus clowns juggling knives sharpened cutthroat suicide universally energetically created.

Birth as an Indigo child co-existing creation:
A Beacon of Light my Child

Beacon of Light

Surprisingly, happiness misunderstood clear to the nonexistence dreamlike state absorbing human beings choosing not to be a Beacon of light for their creation leading a pathway successful evolution of conscious love.

Deteriorating illness bathing in lust envy jealousy hate there are inhumane beings suggesting I am of God a good Christian truth of falsehood. Indigo means leading a road to all that was the oppression programmed virtually expressed generational wholeness completely made up of life to survive.

Washing hands created to fail steppingstones juggling aspirations acknowledging the principle of cause of the effect, nothing happens by chance, it is merely a continuous phenomenon, it be yours twinkling in the distance.

Options are choices we create risking all that filled a cycle shedding the skin of abuse slander your will questioned to survive others choose darkness destructive behavior their life's mission to hurt another soul breathing living to co-exist.

Due to the immediate dismissal of self, old being shredding scales no longer right for causation conscious love brazen apprehensions thrown in the ocean to swim life vest keeping afloat walking all over wellness heal disempowerment higher consciousness.

Flight

Flight is releasing the fears oppressed about yourself by another's hateful projection risking all that use to be dusting off wings ready to fly.

New life new beginnings new conscious love knocking at my door ready as I will be. Here I come Universe catch me I am forever surrendering entrusting our lives in your hands.

Let us FLY!!

Boundaries

Learning new curves and waves through Universal Law, energy affiliated. Famous mediums, psychics, true seekers, and believers, notoriety not of me. Choosing to seek fees as profit are unattended to greed, lacking purpose for services as God's gift transcends.

A conduit of light channeling healing energy, heart seeking transitions, come forth to the existing ascension. Strong energy folds beneath old patterns suggesting the non-ascension categorized as completion.

True to the heart, my heart. Embracing these gifts always hating, not excepting. Hated being different knowing there is more to life. Open channel, information sourced, frightening experiences, ghost, spirits, death and the devil, demons, grotesque images.

Premonitions, future intuition, vibrational channeling, destination begins.

Contact Resource

The author encourages prospects through life's journeys. Feedback is appropriated words carried for miles as is the heart speaks volumes.

What does your heart speak?

Witnessing my experiences based in this book as the lines read appearing faith unrecognizable solely on misguided teachings. Idolization is inappropriate, self-harming growth.

This book is a conversation no one person is comfortable discussing ignoring the true meaning of life. Not certified to suggest any one human being to stop taking medication this worked solely for my transmutation.

Privacy is an important key element for self-resilience passion filled fire. Aura shinning bright challenging fears oppression generationally built imbedded within a sole purpose.

Challenge the idea God consciousness is conscious love. What is the true meaning portrayed by falsehoods? Confident divine masculine and feminine energies in all of humanity.

It is you to choose healing old puss filled wounds growing prosperously challenging nonexistent falsehoods created as fear mongers intoxicating thought process.

Be a solution to the world you choose in **UNITY AS ONE!** Do not be a problem flocking chaos.

In Infinity…

New Chapter to a sequel beginning the true meaning of **LOVE** defined by Divine intervention.

Email: shanarisinganew@yahoo.com

Mystery is important when discussing life and influential energies.

Second Chances

Life and Growth of Self

A second chance of life is when God kicks you in the ass with his big foot from heaven. Gifting you a blessing, even when things did not turn out the way we would want it to be. Blessings occur when we decide to stop and choose not to continue a cycle of bullshit swirling in our heads and hearts.

Choosing to diminish the ultimate sacrifice of self, our old self. Children are the creation God helped create without baggage of hereditary shit. Is this not how we as human beings need to treat each other? In life I have been exhausted to continue solely on old lineage bullshit that has been passed down to me through eras of recycled trauma never ending.

Mental health deteriorates your heart is flooded with the pain of another that is not yours to own nor to embellish the responsibility of unkept falsehoods. As human beings, we must create a barrier for our hearts not allowing venerability, due to the lack of awareness. Manipulation the behavior from our parents, theirs and so forth.

The importance of a child is to uncreate old cycles of loss. To create the wealth of a lineage not superior to another. Only to identify self as you, I, us, not inclusive to them, him, she, he, Non-binary. What is it to me, to create another way of altering another's mindset processing self-growth and healing.

Ambition I carry in my heart to help and honor to change the greater well-being for self is exceptional. However, this exceptionalism of I, not in the sense of ID the ego; lies dormant waiting to be released with grace, self-worth, and confidence.

Confidence carries the heart of a human being embracing all emotional distress forming into emotional intelligence. Believed to be a barrier to self-worth. The outrage of my heart acknowledging who I, my higher self-calls upon an old vessel old thought patterns aligning solely on my inner beauty.

SHANA RISING from the ashes as a Phoenix wilts away. The ashes that once held onto me the inner depths of hell. Old thought patterns reprogramming pain and trauma. Not belonging to my well-being as my mental stability balances confidently expressing passion to ignite advocacy.

Steppingstones to life have curved its way into my path forcing and honoring the fire within. Self-destructive ways of pain swarming, every being I fought to keep balanced from the obstacles forced upon me by another's indiscretions of their own lineage toxic bullshit.

New creation of life in love, I created as a beautiful divine mother in grace. Grace brought upon me God intervening the beauty of creation, thy that is I, higher self.

You and I, as human beings in this place called life. Third dimension ascending to fifth dimensional light being channeling, a conduit life.

Life is in the creation of another's indiscretions implemented by Alpha superior ego of man. Do we end creation as thy mother of self, you and I? That is not true of God ascending his purpose for Mother Mary.

Do my words deviant away from the senseless fear enforced religion subjecting someone else's falsehoods? If it does, that is okay because I do not care about someone else's false belief that has historically harmed the well-being of public health.

Psychological warfare challenges fear and disbelief in self. Alternative thoughts, healthier proclamations. This is the new way of life channeling interferences not of my accountability.

No longer faulting who I am that is made up by parent's who do not take into consideration the faults of abuse, neglect, and sexual incense.

Excuses will always prevail furthering life cycles that will no be acceptable to societal toxicity despairing humanities growth, my growth, my children's growth, and light journey.

Enlightened conduit ready to set flight!

Printed in Great Britain
by Amazon